ES

BUSINESS

ETIQUETTE

Bottom Line Behavior For

Everyday Effectiveness

BY LOU KENNEDY

PALMETTO PUBLISHING

Corpus Christi, Texas

Palmetto Publishing

Library of Congress Cataloging-in-Publication Data

Kennedy, Lou.

ESSENTIAL BUSINESS ETIQUETTE
Bottom line behavior for everyday effectiveness
by Lou Kennedy.

p.   cm.

ISBN 0-9634928-1-0

1. Business etiquette.   2. Office politics.   I. Title.

96-070500 CIP

Printed in the United States of America
2   3   4   5   6   7   8   9   10

This book is dedicated to the four men in my life: Bud, my husband and best friend, and Charles, Michael, and Bennett, our sons. These men acknowledge me as a professional speaker, apply the rules of etiquette in their lives, and encouraged me to write this book.

L.P.K.

CONTENTS

Chapter Three

Chapter Four

Chapter Five

Chapter Six

Chapter Seven

Chapter Eight

Chapter Nine

Chapter Ten

Here's What People Are Saying

About This Book

It's refreshing to see someone take the "mystery" out of corporate manners. Knowing the rules in advance lets us concentrate on building relationships and enhancing our careers, rather than being distracted by which fork to use.

Lou Kennedy gets straight to the heart of corporate manners. She uncovers those mysterious, unspoken rules that we all need to know but that aren't taught in business school.

Michelle Hitt, Past General Plant Manager
Kellogg Company - Memphis, Tennessee

[A] quick and easy reference to etiquette and protocol for the busy professional!

[The book] gives one a reminder of the "little things" that mean "everything" in how one is perceived by others.

I loved your book. It's a valuable resource!

Mary Beth Roach
Roach & Associates - Houston, Texas

The return to the respect of ethics is not only a perceived need in our society, but a mandate for survival! Ethics is played out often through business etiquette. This book is a must for corporations, associations, and a healthy society. It's great!

Naomi R. Rhode
1994 President, National Speakers' Association

This book removes the uncertainty that arises in dealing with many common business situations and relationships. If you don't already have a clear idea of how to behave in a particular situation, this book is good reference material to provide a standard answer to fill the gap in your knowledge.

Ms. Kennedy's book provides good basic fundamentals of appropriate behavior. Using this knowledge, one can confront even the unexpected with more confidence.

William Chriss
Rangel & Chriss, Attorneys - Corpus Christi, Texas

Essential Business Etiquette: Bottom line behavior for everyday effectiveness is a user friendly guide which can be applied to everyday situations... The book contains specific do's and don'ts pertaining to telephone, dress, dining, etc.

Lou, you have raised the consciousness of the men and women that you spoke to.

Larry Clark, Executive Vice President
Puffer Sweiven - Stafford, Texas

It's concise, easy to read, and the format invites use, rather than intimidating the reader. [It's] handy, logical, organized, user friendly, topical, pertinent, [and] valuable to our company.

In our company, most of our managers have been promoted from hourly positions. *Essential Business Etiquette* serves as a valuable reference for people from diverse backgrounds as they move up the career ladder and learn to function in the business world.

Brad Lomax, President
Water Street, Inc. - Corpus Christi, Texas

This book will benefit all who read it. There are numerous practical tips on recurring everyday problems, as well as a reminder to us all to be appreciative of others. No one should be without this handy guide.

Ron Jennings, CPA
Co-author of <u>Employee Theft: How to Spot It</u>
Jennings, Hawley, Cederberg & Co., PC
Corpus Christi, Texas

[This book] puts everything you need to know in one easy-to-read book. Great size to take with you on a business trip. Easy reference book.

We have used the book to help train new employees that meet with the public on proper business etiquette. The book has useful information for secretaries or executives.

Have Lou come speak to your group. She is a wonderful presenter!

Jeanne Tobin
San Jacinto Girl Scouts
Houston, Texas

Your book is concise, but it covers essential information very well!

I like the size because it fits easily into a purse or briefcase without being bulky. The format is easily readable and understandable.

Feedback from students attending the Competitive Edge Workshop has been very positive. The book is included with their workshop materials.

Thank you for developing this much-needed resource in a very "user-friendly" format!

Dr. Kay Clayton
Professor & Dept. Chair, Home Economics
Texas A&M University

INTRODUCTION

ESSENTIAL BUSINESS ETIQUETTE: *Bottom line behavior for everyday effectiveness* is based on my research and observations over fifteen years as a professional speaker and consultant in the field of business and social etiquette. Etiquette reestablished itself in the 1990's as a key component for getting ahead and anchoring oneself in the business world. As we move into the new millennium, many of the former standard rules of business and social etiquette are being rewritten to be more compatible with our rapidly changing times.

An update in etiquette skills is a wise investment of time, whether a person is graduating from college and seeking that first job, whether she is a homemaker entering the work force for the first time, or reentering it after a leave of absence, or whether he or she is a manager or a senior executive.

Say the word "etiquette" rapidly five times. Did you hear the word "ticket" emerge? Webster's Collegiate Dictionary says that etiquette is derived from the French word for ticket. Experience tells us that tickets are necessary to allow entry into a variety of places where we go to be educated and entertained. Tickets usually cost money. How much have you been willing to pay to get where you really wanted to go? Many of our tickets to personal and professional success cost money. Consider how much money was spent on your education. Did you learn enough about etiquette and how to present yourself with confidence? Are you now recognized as a person who knows what to do, when to do it, and how to do it correctly? When it comes to business, do you know someone who lost a promotion or was fired because of inappropriate behavior or bad manners?

The purpose of this book is to provide a quick information reference on business etiquette rules, while also giving suggestions that enhance personal and professional presence and performance. The book is designed for people beginning their careers as well as the busy professionals in the business world who want to know the basic rules of preferred good manners that give them a polished professional edge.

The rules of etiquette help us play the game of "business," with success as the goal. Just as a football coach equips the team players with proper uniforms, the rules of the game, the plays, the objectives of the plays, the discipline of practice, and pep talks before sending the team onto the field to play a winning game, so does the professional person equip himself with the current rules of etiquette and professional image so that he can compete in the field of business.

This book is a "wake-up" call to how we, as individuals and as companies, present ourselves to each other throughout our busy schedules. What does your "physical picture" look like? There is a new casualness in how we dress and entertain, as well as a new informality in how we meet and greet others. Do you know how to use your business card? How do you silently signal a waiter that you have finished your dinner? What message does your telephone voice convey? What kind of first impression do you make? Many business habits practiced in the United States will not impress people in other countries where we are expanding our markets. Knowing about and respecting the cultural diversities of others is critical in building profitable relationships.

Manners are based upon consideration for others. If you want to be recognized as a person who understands and communicates effectively, and as a person who can handle any dining situation gracefully, turn the page. This book is about building personal self - confidence, about being a person with impeccable manners, and a person who applies these skills to enhance his or her financial outcome.

> "Good manners are always important in all contacts in life, but they must spring from real kindness of spirit or they will not ring true."
>
> *-Eleanor Roosevelt*

Chapter One

YOUR WINNING ATTITUDE

"You are only what you are when no one is looking ."

- Robert Soutkey

What do you say to yourself when you wake up and think about your schedule for the day? Do you awake with an attitude of gratitude, or one of grouchiness? Do you want to be associated with yourself all day? Will others want to be associated with you? Attitude is your mental position with regard to facts. It is the way you view things.

What do you do to prepare your attitude for the day? People who are positive in their attitudes and their word choices recognize the benefits of beginning their morning with readings and meditations of positive thoughts. Acknowledge yourself with positive statements about how you look, feel, and think. "Good morning, you beautiful woman/you handsome man! People who work and socialize with you today are going to be glad to spend time with you." These may be the only compliments you receive for the day. Be your own best friend! Contribute to your own happiness and welcome other's contributions as they show up in your day.

Furthermore, your winning attitude shows up as you treat others with courtesy and respect. The behavior of men and women at work is under much scrutiny. Business etiquette in the 1990's has undergone many changes as the number of women competing with men for jobs and promotions has increased.

Yes, this is a decade of transition, when courtesy is an attitude of how one person relates to another person and sex should not be an issue. One of the most sensitive areas in the workplace is the male/female relationship as both sexes strive to establish networks and relationships on a business level. Sexual harassment became an open issue in the 1990's with the confirmation hearings between Anita Hill and Clarence Thomas as well as the Air Force Tail Hook scandal. Strong policy has been written and women (as well as men) are urged to file complaints when they are victims of legitimate harassment. Don't joke about it!

Changing Attitudes

A double standard of attitudes and behavior continues to exist in the workplace. According to Letitia Baldrige's *Complete Guide to Executive Manners,* "people are supposed to treat each other equally and act according to rules of protocol, not of gender; and one sex is supposed to come to the aid of the other whenever either needs assistance."

Baldrige says that the "polished professional," whether a man or a woman:

• Moves quickly to open a door for anyone walking who has his or her hands full.

• Picks up whatever someone else has dropped who cannot retrieve it as easily as he or she can.

• Stands to greet a visitor to the meeting in his or her office.

• Assists a colleague struggling to get in or out of his or her coat.

This attitude of behavior makes common sense, yet it is still more theory than fact, according to research conducted by Jan Yager, author of *Business Protocol: How to Survive and Succeed in Business.* (copyright 1991)

According to Yager, " ... there are still relatively few women in top management because men and women have not yet found ways to feel comfortable working together at high levels without compromising ingrained views of the right way to treat one another."

According to research reported on by The National Foundation for Women Business Owners in March of 1996, one of every four American workers is employed by a business owned by women. California has the largest number of women-owned businesses, followed by Texas.

Men Working for Female Bosses

Women who work with men working under them have created the need for a new set of attitudes and rules on how to work together. Behavior that helps to minimize possible embarrassment and conflict on the job is discussed in *The Complete Office Handbook,* by office expert Mary A. DeVries. She makes the following suggestions:

> • Avoid offers of help that have sexual connotations, such as, "Since you're a woman, you'll need help from a man. Feel free to call on me."

> • Let your boss indicate whether your relationship will be formal or informal.

> • Do not misinterpret her friendliness as a romantic overture.

> • Allow your boss to set the time and pace for work-related duties.

> • Treat her with the same respect you would grant a male executive.

A woman working for a female boss should not change her behavior from that she would exhibit toward a male boss. The best rule of thumb is to treat an executive according to the etiquette appropriate to the position and not to let the gender influence your behavior and attitude.

Six Attitudes Worth Remembering

"It's your attitude, not your aptitude that determines your altitude."

Zig Zigler

1. Your attitude towards people influences your behavior. It is not always possible to camouflage how you feel.

2. Your attitude determines the level of your job satisfaction.

3. Your attitude affects everyone who comes in contact with you, at the office, in a meeting, on the telephone or at lunch.

4. Your attitude is reflected in the tone of your voice, by the way you stand and move, in your facial expressions, and through other nonverbal messages you send.

5. Your attitude is adjustable. You have choices regarding the attitude that you display.

6. Choose to be a person of positive attitudes. If you do, you will enhance the environment.

Attitude

"The longer I live, the more I realize the impact of attitude on life. Attitude, to me, is more important than education, than money, than circumstances, than failures, than successes, than what other people think or say or do. It is more important than appearance, giftedness or skill. It will make or break a company, ...an organization...a home. The remarkable thing is we have a choice every day regarding the attitude we will embrace for that day. We cannot change our past...we cannot change the fact that people will act a certain way. We cannot change the inevitable. The only thing we can do is play the one string we have, and it is our attitude...I am convinced that life is 10% what happens to me and 90% how I react to it. And so it is with you...we are in charge of our Attitudes."

Author Unknown

Your Professional Image

2

The professional image that a person projects begins with the exterior packaging, extending from one's hair to his or her shoes. In the highly competitive job market, a well-groomed person has the immediate visual advantage. One assumes that anyone who can package himself in a manner appropriate to a job position can also handle meticulous details relating to the job. People who effectively project the professional image even command higher starting salaries than those who do not.

First Impressions

You never get a second chance to make a first impression. It takes ten to fifteen seconds to make a first impression. If you create a negative impression, it could take as many as ten additional encounters to change that opinion! How many people get that opportunity? So ask yourself, " What visual image do I project?" Ninety-three percent of the impression you make on others is based on what they see. The clothes you wear and how you wear them are absolutely vital to your total appearance and to the attitude you project. Until another form of communication takes place, perception is reality. Therefore, it is in your best interest to know what your picture looks like. The key to successful and appropriate dressing begins with paying attention to what the successful people in your profession wear on a regular basis. The well-groomed business person pays attention to details. Although you may not be able to afford the finest quality in fabrics, you can copy the styling of the garments worn by those above you. It is important to remember to dress to suit the decision makers in the company who are in control of your career advancements.

To assure that you create a positive first impression, make an entrance walking with purposeful steps, begin your conversation with words of praise or thanks and make sure that your grooming is beyond reproach.

Chewing gum, tobacco, or smoking cigarettes does nothing to enhance your visual image. It creates a negative first impression.

> "Always be a first rate version of yourself instead of a second rate version of someone else."
>
> *Judy Garland*

The Businessman's Appearance

> "You always make some kind of statement, powerful or inept, with the way you dress.."
>
> *-Robert Pante*

When it comes to clothes, people tend to judge the wearer's status, character and abilities based on what they see. Suits are the foundation of a business wardrobe. Fabrics, fit and fashion are important to consider when investing in this business outfit.

Whether buying a traditional, tailored suit or a jacket and slacks for the business casual look, fabrics made of natural fibers are preferable to synthetics because they "breathe," hold their shape, move with the body, and send a message that signifies quality. With your climates in mind, choose from wool, tropical wools, gabardine, cottons and linens. There are some finely made polyesters that have the advantage of staying wrinkle free - a real plus when travelling. Invest in suits appropriate to your profession – suits that have long - lasting style and can be "dressed up or down" with creative accessories.

Fit is critical to a suit jacket and pants. The jacket should fit comfortably across the shoulders with no pulling or wrinkles. The sleeves should hang midway through the wrist bone to allow for a half-inch shirt cuff to show from under the coatsleeve. The jacket should be long enough to rest in your bent fingers when they are in a cupped position under the bottom of the jacket. It should also be long enough to cover the full seat of the pants.

Fashion in suit designs will periodically change. Stay current with lapel widths, single or double-breasted jackets, two or three buttons, single or double vents. The choice of cuffed or uncuffed pants is dictated by the person's height. The shorter man may prefer no cuff, giving the illusion of added height.

Suit tips: Tall men look good in dark colored suits without bold stripes or patterns to accentuate their height. A double-breasted jacket with a vented back is a fashionable look for a tall man of slender to medium build.

• Heavy-set men should opt for dark colored suits with stripe and a non-vented back. If choosing a two button suit, only button the top button.

• Shorter men look best in monochromatic dark colored, pinstripe suits that appear to add height.

• Color is an important and interesting component of the business suit. Research shows that dark blue and dark gray are the most authoritative colors, and that they are also flattering to everyone. The dark blue pinstripe suit communicates the greatest degree of authority. A well-balanced wardrobe includes a lightweight summer gabardine suit in a shade of tan, a navy blue blazer, and grey and khaki slacks. Work with an experienced tailor for a comfortable fit in sleeve and trouser lengths.

Tip: for single-breasted jackets: Remember to button your jacket when standing and walking, and unbutton it when sitting. A double-breasted jacket looks best when it is worn closed.

A white, cotton pocket handkerchief adds another visual accent detail to a jacket. Silk pocket squares come in many choices of color and patterns and look best when they complement, but do not match, the tie.

Shirts do make a definite statement. A starched, white, long-sleeved, 100% cotton broadcloth shirt is the favorite in the business world. An off-white or ecru color is flattering to men with a sallow complexion. The fit of a shirt collar is important to the well-tailored look. You should be able to comfortably fit two fingers between the collar and your neck. The long-sleeved shirt should extend no more than half an inch beyond the sleeve of your jacket.

If you are working in your office without your jacket, put it on whenever your boss, an outside client or customer, or anyone of importance from the outside comes into your office. This is a sign of courtesy.

Pockets serve the specific purpose of holding a pen and/or pencil, but choose a writing instrument that will not project bulk across the chest.

Pocket tip: Do not carry your colored memo messages in your shirt pocket.

Ties show up as personality statements that are noticed and remembered. Silk ties are the best choice for their versatility, elegance, and correctness. A tie wardrobe should include conservative foulard and paisley patterns, diagonal stripes, and polka dots. The 1990's brought an additional flourish of bold patterns, designs and colors that are worn by men in many different professions.

Tie Tip: The tip of the tie should reach the center of the belt buckle, with the outer two tips at the top of the trouser waistband. The shirt buttons should not be seen. Stand up straight and check your tie in front of the mirror. The standard "four-in-hand" is the most popular knot to wear.

Shoes send a strong message about a person and should never be overlooked. Whether you are a corporate male who chooses a laced, plain-toe oxford or a professional man who wears a plain or tasseled loafer, buy shoes of good quality leather. Black, brown and cordovan are acceptable colors for daytime business. Shoes should always be highly polished. Worn-down heels should be replaced, and bottoms should be half-soled when they begin to wear thin. The life of good leather shoes can be lengthened with professional care at a good shoe shop. For a more casual shoe, some men bring out a pair of Hush Puppies or oxfords for a revival of old standbys.

Socks should complement the trouser color by extending into the shoe. The sock should extend upward over the calf so that a man's leg skin and hair are not visible when the trouser leg rides up. Traditional solid colors of black, brown, grey and navy have been joined by tailored patterned socks that lend a dash of "punch and flair" to the sock. Some men have allergic reactions to the dye in colored socks. Try a silk liner sock underneath a lightweight colored sock in order to complement the trouser. White athletic socks should be worn only with tennis clothes, on the golf course, or with athletic wear. They are a no-no for business wear.

Belts, in plain leather or reptile, should be black or cordovan, one inch wide. A plain brass buckle and no weight-gain marks along the belt notches are part of a "polished" look. Keep the shirt placket, tie, and belt buckle in a straight line.

Accessories are another important and noticeable part of the businessman's wardrobe. Writing pens and pencils of excellent quality are carried inside either a jacket pocket or in a shirt pocket. A fine wristwatch, (not digital), a wedding band, and plain gold cuff links are additional parts of a man's accessories. A leather wallet should be slim and should lie flat in the jacket or trouser pocket. A dark leather briefcase or leather-bound pad completes the look of an organized professional. Always replenish your supply of business cards before leaving your home or office. Do not be caught without cards if you own them.

Hair styles and lengths for businessmen vary over the years. Sideburns come and go in popularity. Most companies and corporations have specific guidelines to follow regarding the accepted length of men's hair around the shirt collar. Male executives are usually expected to wear their hair above the neck of the shirt or suit collar. A businessman with long hair slicked back in a pony tail is often more acceptable in the arts and entertainment industries. Men enjoy expressing their individuality in hair styles; short hair is not the only choice available in many job dress codes.

Facial hair is usually discouraged in the corporate sector, but when beards and mustaches are worn, they should be clipped and neat at all times. Attention should also be directed to the trimming of nose and ear hairs.

Smiles increase your face value and do not cost you one cent. It takes only fourteen facial muscles to smile, while seventy-two muscles are required to frown. Of all the things you wear, your expression is the most important. Smile!

Colognes and fragrances are another signature of individuality. Be remembered for a clean smell that does not overpower others or cause an allergy reaction due to heavy application. An effective deodorant to control body odor should be used every day. Apply a little to your palms if they tend to sweat.

In addition to the traditional business look, there are occasions where casual attire is appropriate. Exactly what does the term "business casual" mean? Tattered blue jeans, tee shirts, dirty tennis shoes or loafers with no socks are not what is meant by casual dress in most businesses. Docker slacks, worn with a belt, are an appropriate replacement for tailored suit slacks. A sport coat or sweater with a polo shirt, a band collar shirt, a turtleneck, a plaid shirt or a denim shirt all fall under the "casual dress" description.

THE BUSINESSWOMAN'S APPEARANCE

Career women have moved away from the rigid dress codes of the '80s. Women no longer feel the need to dress like men in pinstripe suits with a necktie or bow or to soften the somber look with a lace handkerchief or lace bodysuit. Women understand how to put together an authoritative, professional image that looks credible as well as feminine.

The corporate woman knows that black, grey and navy are considered the best power colors. The matched skirted suit is the universally accepted look. A beautifully constructed, fully lined suit in black is the anchor to an executive woman's wardrobe. A silk blouse in white or ivory speaks for authority, while a colored, challis print will give a softer, but still professional, look. Necklines should be conservative in cut and designed to look tailored when accessorized with jewelry. Red is an energy color and a favorite for women. Red is also visible and memorable. A well-cut jacket or blazer in red wool gabardine may be paired with a straight, black wool gabardine skirt and white silk blouse for a sharp business look. Herringbone and small plaid patterns are popular in suits and coat dresses.

When working in a suit in your office, the jacket may be removed. Put it on when your boss, an outside client, customer, or someone of importance from the outside enters your office. Suit jacket pockets are a convenient place to carry business cards. I put ten business cards in all of my jacket pockets at the beginning of each week so that I am seldom caught without one.

Professional women not in a traditional corporate environment are enjoying more color, such as teal, periwinkle, and dark green in their suits. More business-women in the '90s are dressing for themselves, with confidence in their appearance and their professional abilities.

The dress has taken its rightful place in the business world and fits right in with a sophisticated and authoritative style. A long-sleeved coat dress with metal or bone buttons projects an air of authority. A tailored dress with a jacket is another option. This look holds its own professional edge in the company of blazers and skirts. Hemlines go up and down the leg like a designer yo-yo. The consistently preferred length is between an inch above to an inch or so below the knee. Shorter skirts come and go in popularity and demand a shapely leg and full attention to posture, especially when sitting. Secure slip straps so that they will not show. Check slip length to assure that your slip is not longer than your skirt. Matching hosiery to the skirt color and shoes provides a monochromatic look for the woman whose job allows a variety in styles and lengths. Carry an extra pair of hosiery in your briefcase. A run in your stockings ruins your professional appearance and creates stress when you least want it.

Periodically, fashion designers create very tailored pantsuits for businesswomen. The menswear look with a dramatic suit lapel pin or beautiful scarf can create a powerfully feminine effect. With casual dress becoming a norm in many industries, a pantsuit or good-looking slacks, with a shirt, sweater or jacket create a polished appearance for the office. If it is appropriate in her work environment, a woman could consider wearing pants on the job if she meets the following criteria:

• She has a great figure for pants and does not accentuate it by wearing tight fitting pants.

• She has good fashion sense and knows what jacket style complements the pants.

• She can afford good quality fabrics and well-tailored suits.

Accessories add color and variety to the power colors. Beautiful silk scarves in various sizes may be worn as an accent at the neck of a suit. Make sure that the scarf is anchored securely so that you do not have to constantly adjust it throughout the day. Pearls are always in good taste. As First Lady, Barbara Bush made the three-strand pearls a popular choice for many women. One piece of jewelry should be a focal point, whether it is pearls, a gold or silver choker, a chain, or a large pin. The motto "Less is best" is still worth remembering. A watch for business and corporate wear should be void of gems and have a leather or metal band. Bracelets should be a good quality and limited in number. When they clink together they are annoying to others, even if they do not bother the woman wearing them. The number of rings should be limited also. A woman may wear her wedding rings on her left hand and one quality ring on her right hand. If you are someone who enjoys wearing a ring on four fingers of one hand, consider doing this after work, in your social and leisure time.

Shoes of good quality leather are an important wardrobe investment. The life of an expensive shoe is extended by professional polishing and by attention to heel tips and soles. Heel heights vary with women and professions. A conservative, corporate heel is around two inches. Black, navy, taupe, burgundy and brown are the necessary colors in your shoe wardrobe. Closed heel and toe signifies a conservative look. Women in creative jobs have more flexibility in shoe color and design. An ankle bracelet is not a standard accessory for business-women.

Purses and briefcases should be of good quality leather. Your purse wardrobe should include a small purse that fits into your briefcase and can hold a lipstick, comb, credit and business cards, and keys. Whenever possible, a purse needs to sit on your lap during a business lunch. It is best not to put it on the floor, on the back of your chair, in the chair next to you, or on the table.

REMEMBER THE BASICS OF GROOMING

A hair style should be appropriate to a woman's face and should focus attention on the face. Once her hair is fixed in the morning, a woman should not be a slave to it all day. A professional look is short, just above the shoulders or, if longer, pulled back from the face. Hair ornaments should be tailored for business hours.

Makeup enhances a woman's skin tones and color. The goal is to wear makeup without looking overly made up. Consult a professional cosmetologist for help in selecting colors that look good on you. Lipstick should be blotted before a businesswoman goes out to eat. Lipstick prints on cups and glasses are unsightly and the lipstick alters the taste of the beverage.

Fragrance is a very personal part of women's and men's wardrobes and images. Many people do not feel fully clothed without fragrance. Just remember when applying fragrance that it does not appeal to all people. I have seen people move away from someone who is wearing too much fragrance. Some people experience allergic reactions to fragrance. Therefore, I advise pro-fessional women and men to apply colognes and eau de toilettes sparingly for business wear. Save the heavier fragrances for social occasions.

Is it proper for a woman to put on lipstick in public? Business protocol suggests that, when commonality has been apparent throughout the meal, now is not the time to stand out. Apply lipstick in the restroom. A group of women having lunch together may choose to apply lipstick quickly, without needing to pull out a mirror. If you are the guest, take your cue from the hostess.

The corporate woman's fingernails are best worn slightly longer that her finger tips and colored with clear polish. A French manicure is also appropriate. The professional woman who wears nail color should have beautifully manicured nails and should check them daily for chips. She must also pay close attention not to mar her business cards with her nail color.

Breath mints are readily available to a considerate professional. Coffee and lunch breath need to be re-freshed during the day. Those who come in contact with you notice, even if you don't. Chewing gum is not an image enhancer. If you chew gum as a breath freshener or cigarette substitute, do so in private.

> "The body is the shell of the soul and dress the husk of that shell; but the husk often tells what the kernel is."
>
> *-Anonymous*

Chapter three

COMMUNICATING EFFECTIVELY

3

Communicating is a two-part process which takes place when information is exchanged, understanding is promoted, and questions are answered. The process requires participation between a speaker/sender and listener/receiver. Each party must participate since true communication depends on it.

We send messages:
- through the spoken word.
- with body gestures that communicate our message to the listener's eyes.
- through the written word.
- through touch.

We receive messages:
- through listening.
- through observing.
- through touch.

You cannot avoid communicating. However, the quality of a person's communication depends upon the level of his commitment to the process.

The Art of Making Conversation

"A good conversationalist is not one who remembers what was said, but who says what someone wants to remember."

-John Mason Brown

Conversation is an important part of one's business presence, and conversation enhances both the personal and the corporate image. Anyone in business who is at ease with conversation is an asset to the company, both inside and outside the office.

Conversational Aptitudes

A good conversationalist is polite and cares about other people. He is well- informed and can talk on a variety of subjects. He can move the conversation through topics to suit the person or group participating in the conversation. He includes others and does not monopolize the conversation. He knows the value of eye contact and uses it consistently as he gives you quality attention. He does not interrupt, nor does he correct another's grammar or pronunciation in public. He knows how to accept and pay compliments gracefully.

Subjects to Avoid

"To speak kindly does not hurt the tongue."

-Proverb

A skilled conversationalist understands that certain subjects are best avoided in casual conversation with people one does not know well.
- Her health or that of other people.
- Controversial issues that could result in emotional differences of opinion.
- Stories in questionable taste.
- Gossip that is harmful to people, personally or professionally.
- Personal misfortunes.
- A person's age and income.

Working a Room

Whether you are attending a Chamber of Commerce function, a convention, a trade show, or a social event, the art of "small talk" is regarded as an important business skill. Many have said, "It's not what you know, but who you know." Small talk should intrigue, delight, amuse and fill up time pleasantly. It's purpose is to put people at ease - not to teach, preach or impress. People who appear at ease in conversation attract others to them like a magnet.

Utilizing the "Big Five W's" will make small talk easy. You probably know them already. WHO, WHAT, WHEN, WHERE and WHY are the openers to sentences that will get you into a casual conversation with ease.. HOW is another sentence opener that can be used effectively. Ask a question beginning with any one of these words. Be sure to make it an open ended question - one that can not be answered by "Yes" or "No." The questions should be relevant to the function you are attending.

Here are a few examples of situations and questions you might ask.

• "There certainly are alot of people here at this fund-raiser. How long have you been involved with the American Cancer Society? What made you decide to support this organization with your dollars and your time?"

• "That was a lovely wedding! How long have you known the bride and groom? Where are they planning to live after they return from their honeymoon?"

• "These Chamber of Commerce functions seem to be attracting new members. What company are you with? How many of these evening functions have you attended? What do you enjoy most about them?"

Be aware of body language when visiting in mixed company. Use caution with flirting in a business setting. What you may regard as friendly banter may be interpreted by others as a "come-on."

When "working a room" and making "small talk," do not ask a professional for detailed information or advice. Ask for a business card and say that you will be calling his or her office to make an appointment to discuss some business matters.

Making Lively Conversation

Six keys to lively conversation are covered in the book, *How To Work A Room,* by Susan Roane. She makes the following suggestions:

1. Read one newspaper a day - information is power.

2. Clip and collect articles and cartoons. If you have an article on file that you can send someone that relates to a conversation, it creates another way to be remembered.

3. Read newsletters and professional journals whenever possible before going to an organization's function.

4. Take notes on other people's clever remarks and stories. They can be good conversation openers.

5. Use humor as a special way of bringing people together. It establishes rapport and warmth among people.

6. Listen actively to others words, concentrate on them, and respond accordingly.

Communication is a two-party process. When you do your part, you will find that most people will respond in kind.

"Wear a smile and have friends; wear a frown and have wrinkles. What do we live for if not to make the world less difficult for each other?"

-George Eliot

Little Things Make a Difference

Many people say that they are working harder at their job and enjoying it less. David Letterman was talking about this on his television show and said, "The quality of consideration of others is deteriorating." Consideration of your fellow workers will be appreciated by them.

"Please" and "Thank you" are words worth using for actions large and small. Opening a door, helping to carry a heavy load, and paying a compliment when it is due or unexpected all help brighten someone's busy day.

"You cannot do a kindness too soon, for you never know how soon it will be too late."

-Ralph Waldo Emerson

THE ART OF PUBLIC SPEAKING

Public speaking is the number one fear of most people, according to *People's Almanac Presents the Book of Lists.* Most people are not comfortable with having to get up in front of a group to give a report, much less to give a speech. However, you really are practicing public speaking skills all day as you go about your business and as you speak to other people.

If you want to be taken seriously, learn how to use your voice effectively. Thirty-eight percent of the way you influence others has to do with the way you use your voice. Do you know how you sound? Are you a mumbler, a slow talker, a fast talker or a screecher? Do you sound as good as you look? Just as the quality of your handshake pleases the sense of touch and the quality of your clothing pleases the eye, so should the quality of your voice please the ear.

Speak into a tape recorder as you read a paragraph out loud. Listen to your voice with a critical ear.

• *Pitch* should hit a midline between high and low. Newscasters are experts at this. Women need to listen carefully to their pitch since many women have a higher natural pitch than most men. Add a level of excitement to this voice and it can sound shrill. When you find a pitch that sounds pleasing to your ear, practice moving it above and below that point to create an interesting sound and to avoid a monotone pitch.

• *Rate of speech* is important. Most professional speakers, actors, and other performers speak at a rate of 125 to 150 words per minute. They vary the rate when they want to emphasize a point and keep the listener interested.

• *Inflection* is the way you change the pitch of your voice to show different emotions behind your words. Tape your voice inflection as you say, "Be home by seven o'clock" with anger, friendliness, the suggestion of a pleasant surprise. Do you hear the difference in meaning of the same spoken words? Pay particular attention to inflection at the end of a sentence and the meaning you wish to convey.

• *Resonance* is a term referring to the fullness of the voice. To produce that sound, breathe deeply from the diaphragm. This will also calm your nerves. If your voice produces a nasal sound, open your mouth wider as you speak.

The words we speak account for only seven percent of the way we influence others. Expand your vocabulary so that your text is interesting. Eliminate non-words and slang words that act as a crutch in your presentation. Interjecting the words "like," "you know," "okay" and "so" for space fillers between your thoughts reduce the power of your message.

• *Rehearsal* will raise your level of confidence and lower your level of nervousness. It is perfectly natural for you to experience a "rush hour traffic jam of butterflies" in your stomach before giving a speech. Deep breathing through your nose and exhaling through your mouth helps to release tension. Exercising prior to a presentation will reduce physical tension, while also energizing your body.

• *Visualization* is the process of creating a vivid mental picture of yourself standing in front of the audience. Picture yourself relaxed and confident, filled with enthusiasm and ready to go. Your audience is ready to listen and support you. Feel your stance, hear your steady voice, see your gestures. Imagine a responsive audience and a good Q & A before you close. Feel the satisfaction of a job well done.

The time has come. Your name is called and you feel yourself moving toward the lectern.

When You Are the Introducer :

• Move with energy in your step, confidence in your posture, and a smile on your face (unless this is a solemn occasion).

• Acknowledge your audience with your eyes and smile.

• Distribute your weight evenly with your feet placed about a shoulder's width apart.

• Adjust the microphone so that it will be the right height for you.

• Speak directly into the microphone from a distance of four to six inches.

• When speaking in a noisy environment, get very close to the microphone.

• If you are using notes, place them where you want them before you start to speak.

• Highlight information about the speaker's background.

• Do not use parts of the speaker's past speeches that you have heard. She may be planning to use them in this speech too.

• Be enthusiastic. The introducer sets the audience's mood before they welcome the speaker to the stage.

• Do not draw attention to negative conditions existing in the room, such as strange table arrangements, difficulty in seeing the speaker, room temperature, or noise from the auction being held in the banquet room across the hall.

• Be brief! Do not deviate from the prepared introduction if one is provided for you by the speaker's staff. An introducer who talks for ten to fifteen minutes takes away from the speaker's time.

When You Are the Speaker :

Follow the first seven steps as listed for the introducer. Also:

• Graciously acknowledge your introducer and call him or her by name.

• If you need to keep up with your time, put your watch in your pocket so that you can easily place it on the lectern with your notes. If your audience sees you looking at your watch on your wrist, they may start focusing on their own watches.

• Never apologize for how nervous you are; never say that you really are prepared but are scared to death.

• Memorize your opening statements so that you are not reading from your notes initially.

• Keep your hands relaxed when they are visible on the lectern. White-knuckle gripping of the lectern tells the audience that you are very uncomfortable.

• Direct your eye contact toward one person for about five seconds, and then move on to another person. This helps you feel as though you are engaged in a one-on-one conversation.

• Never focus on a spot over the audience's heads. They will feel that you do not care about them, and therefore they will not care for you!

• Focus your attention on your listeners and your message, and you will forget yourself.

Preparation + Practice = Peak Performance

The Art of Listening

"Silence is one great art of conversation."

-William Hazlitt

You are called upon to listen to others any time that you are not alone. Large or small amounts of information are mentally stored when you are interested in the speaker's words. You can also be extremely bored when you are not interested. The Chinese character for listening includes symbols for the ears, the eyes and the heart.

Consider the benefits of listening with purpose:

• You acknowledge others and often increase their self-esteem.

• You acknowledge yourself and learn a consider able amount about how you think and feel when you listen to yourself.

• You create a space for the release of tension and stress through the constructive sharing of thoughts and ideas.

• You earn respect and loyalty from those who work with you.

• You increase your ability to negotiate.

Communicate that you are listening. Facial expressions with good eye contact will let the speaker know whether you are interested, bored, confused, sympathetic or in agreement. Attitudes communicated through body positions will show whether you are relaxed, stressed, insecure, nervous, suspicious or defensive.

A person who concentrates as he listens is giving the gift of self to another person. This gift is appreciated and does not go unnoticed.

The Art of Correspondence

Correct correspondence etiquette is a part of your professional image which becomes a visual extension of yourself. Your stationery should be congruent with your business correspondence needs, and should include official business stationery, informal business stationery and informal note cards.

Official Business Letter Form

Full Block, the most commonly used style, begins to the extreme left of the page. Place the date two to four lines beneath the letterhead. Begin the address three to eight lines below the date.

The Address Should Include:

1. Addressee's courtesy title and full name with correct spelling.

2. Business title or department.

3. Full name of business.

4. Street address plus suite number; separate the two with a comma or two spaces. Write out the word Suite. Place it on the line above if there are too many words for one line.

5. City, state and zip code - Abbreviate the name of the state with caps and no period.

6. Use the PO Box if it is given as well as the street address. The letter will arrive sooner.

7. Write out streets named First through Twelfth; thereafter, use Arabic numbers.

8. On the inside address, spell out Street, Parkway or Avenue. Boulevard may be abbreviated to Blvd.

The salutation is placed two to four lines beneath the address, again staying flush left. Use a colon in a typed letter and a comma in a handwritten letter.

The paragraphs in the body of the letter are not indented, and there should be a double space between paragraphs.

The closing is placed two lines below the last line of the body. Most business closings carry one word, such as, "Sincerely" or "Cordially." If you chose to add the word yours, do not capitalize it unless it comes first. Reserve the words "Cordially" or "Regards" in your closing for people with whom you are on a first-name basis.

Your name in type appears four to six lines below the closing. Your handwritten signature goes in that space. When the company name is in the letterhead, you will not use it in the signature.

A women who wishes to be called Mrs. instead of Ms. should indicate this before her typewritten name, as (Mrs.) Sarah Wells.

Your degrees belong after your typed last name if they do not appear on the letterhead. They do not follow your handwritten signature.

Effective Letter Writing Tips

An effective letter can influence others. This influence comes both from attention to the appearance of the text and from the way the words are used.

Remember the Following Pointers:

- Have a strong sense of purpose about a letter before writing it.

- Limit your letter to one page.

- Get to the point early.

- Emphasize the reader's perspective ..."What's in it for me?"

- Avoid beginning a paragraph with: I, We, My, or Our.

- Limit your sentences to twenty-two words or less.
- Use active verbs.
- Keep your words to a maximum of three syllables.
- Never write in anger.
- Be creative to make your letters stand out from others.
- End with an action step that suggests the reader's next move or yours.

The Informal Business Letter

The informal business letter is different from the formal business letter in five ways.

1. It is typed on monarch or half-sheet stationery.

2. The date is placed in the upper right hand corner.

3. The salutation is placed 2 to 5 spaces below the date line and flush left on the page.

4. The close and signature are on the right side of the page lined up under the date.

5. The addressee's address may appear flush left and 2 to 5 spaces below the final signature line.

Handwritten Personal Letter

A handwritten note may be short and to the point. A note is preferred when the subject is congratulations, appreciation, thanks, apology or condolence. Make sure that the spelling and grammar are correct and that the writing is legible. A man should not have his secretary write his thank-you notes.

Write a Note

- When you receive a written invitation with no request for a response.
- When you have been to a cocktail or dinner party.

• When you have been a houseguest for a weekend or longer.

• When you receive a gift. (Take a moment to personalize the message by stating how or where you will use the gift.)

• When a friend or associate has been promoted, a note of congratulations is in order.

• When a friend or associate has had a death in his or her family.

• When a friend or associate celebrates a marriage, the birth or adoption of a child, or some special recognition.

Business Cards

Your business card is another written extension of your image and your company. The text, type and graphics should communicate the image of the business. Knowing how and when to present your card contributes to your professional presence.

• Attach your card to a presentation folder or literature if you are giving a presentation. Some people in your audience may not be familiar with you or the company that you represent.

• Carry enough cards with you to meet the needs of the occasion. It helps to put at least ten cards in a pocket of suit jackets that you frequently wear.

• Exchange cards at business/social gatherings you attend. Do not automatically assume that everyone wants or needs your card. Talk to people for a few minutes before offering yours or asking for theirs.

• Keep your cards clean and protected from creases. If your card becomes soiled or tattered, it is best to discard it rather than hand out a negative image.

• Produce your card quickly and easily from your pocket or purse.

• When you are handed a business card, read it carefully and make a complimentary statement about it. Holding the card as you speak instead of immediately putting it away suggests a nonverbal sign of respect.

• Personalize your card if the occasion warrants. Draw one diagonal line through your name on the front of the card. On the back, write a brief message and sign your first name only.

• Do not substitute a check book deposit blank for your business card.

• Do not use someone else's card (because you ran out of your own) and write your message on the back to give to a third party. You don't know which side will be displayed in the Rolodex.

The Art of Touch

Phrases such as "Give me five" and "Press the flesh" refer to physical touch. The handshake is the most acceptable and appreciated sign of business greeting in the United States.

Businesswomen do not want to be hugged, kissed, or patted when doing business with men. The "brother-sister greeting kiss" is often misconstrued.

Air-kissing, where a woman puckers up her lips and puts her cheek alongside someone else's cheek, looks like a phony, awkward gesture.

Men have slapped each other on the back in a gesture of congratulations for decades. Women use words and handshakes.

"What you are shouts so loud in my ears that I cannot hear what you say."

-Ralph Waldo Emerson

Chapter Four

INVITATIONS AND GIFT GIVING

Invitations

Americans are hopelessly remiss when it comes to responding to invitations, whether at a social or business level. Not to respond borders on rudeness to the host and hostess and makes their job of ordering the food and drink for a party difficult. This usually results in an unnecessary expense to the host.

Guidelines on When to Mail Your Invitations

• When inviting executives from other cities to an important conference or seminar: mail invitations six to eight months before the event.

• Invitations for an important dinner with out-of-town guests: mail four to six months before the dinner.

• Luncheon invitations : three to five weeks before the date.

• Tea party: two to three weeks.

• Breakfast for a large group: two to four weeks.

• Cocktail party: two to four weeks.

• Evening reception which will take place before or after another event: two to four weeks.

Responding to Invitations

RSVP is a call for a response to an invitation and is written on the lower left-hand corner of the invitation. The response should be made within twenty-four hours, if possible, and no later than one week. It is rude to cancel an acceptance for any reason other than an emergency. It is equally rude to send someone in your place if the host is expecting you. Do not bring uninvited guests with you. A response is not necessary to a party for which you are asked to pay money for tickets or auctions. ("RSVP," "R.S.V.P" or "R.s.v.p.")

When "Regrets Only" is written in the lower left-hand corner of an invitation, followed by a telephone number, a reply is requested only if you do not plan to attend.

Many business invitations include an RSVP card for the prospective guests' use in responding. The host company may choose to stamp the RSVP envelope or leave that detail to the invited guest.

If an executive is away on an extended trip, his secretary should handle the RSVPs. If the secretary knows the host well, a short note stating that her boss is out of town should accompany the RSVP card.

Tip: If RSVP is not motivating your guest to respond, change your verbage. _Example-_ Please declare your intention.

Gift Giving

Knowing what gift to give and when to give it is part of the protocol of business gift-giving. Some companies have a no-gifts policy and this policy must be honored. Some people expect gifts, some believe they deserve them, and others might see gift-giving as an inappropriate gesture.

Before purchasing a gift, check with the intended receiver's company policy to find out if any price limits are set. If so, adhere to them. Never give a gift as a direct thank you for the receipt of an order or purchase. It is appropriate to send a gift to a business colleague's spouse and children when celebrations such as weddings, graduations, etc. occur. Send a gift shortly after receiving the invitation or announcement. Do not wait for six moths after the event to respond.

When company policy does not allow the acceptance of gifts, ask if invitations to dinner or the theater are permissible. When policy restrictions prevent all of these gestures of appreciation, a handwritten letter will allow you to express your appreciation. Do not say that you would have preferred to have given a gift, but were restricted by company policy.

Selecting a Gift

Use your creativity when selecting gifts. Think about each recipient and what you know about his or her individual interests, hobbies and enthusiasms.

A book relating to the recipient's interests will be appreciated. A personally autographed copy of the book becomes a treasured gift. An unusual arrangement of exotic flowers could be a memorable gift. Gift baskets of gourmet pastas, sauces, cheeses and crackers, candies, coffees, teas, or wines will delight most recipients. A gift (such as golf balls, fishing tackle, or cyclist or skier's accessories) which relates to the recipient's special interests is useful and appreciated.

If you are giving a gift to a person from another country or of another culture, do some research into what is considered an acceptable gift.

Less personal choices for clients you do not know well might include a business card case, a glass paperweight, or an electronic gadget.

Price Guidelines for Gift Purchasing:

- Ten to twenty-five dollars for your manager.
- Twenty-five to fifty dollars for a CEO or upper-level executive.
- Ten to twenty-five dollars for client gifts.
- Fifty to one hundred dollars for the executive-to-executive level.
- Gifts whose value is more than one hundred dollars are for very important people and occasions.

You are expected or obligated to give tangible gifts for certain events, and the financial cost will vary with each occasion. Some of the most delightful gifts to receive come for no special reason, but are simply a gesture of friendship.

Chapter Five

BUSINESS DINING SKILLS

5

There are many rules to be learned when it comes to the art of dining. Some benefits of putting these rules into practice include:

- Having self-confidence at any place setting, from casual to formal.

- Being able to focus your attention on those dining with you, whether for business or social purposes.

- Passing the dining test at a job interview meal.

The Invitation Before Dining

When You Invite a Client to Meet You:

- Choose two or three dates and let the client select.

- Select two restaurants where you are comfortable and ask client to choose.

- You are responsible for making the reservation.

- Clear your calendar to accommodate the engagement.

- Reconfirm the time and place with the client or the secretary on the morning of a lunch meeting, or the afternoon before a breakfast meeting.

- If your meeting must be rescheduled, be sure to call the restaurant and cancel your reservation.

- The person who extends the invitation expects to pay the bill.

When You Are the Invited Guest:

- If you are unable to keep the appointment, make the call yourself. Do not have a secretary make the call for you and do not leave the message on an answering machine.

- Remember that the person who extended the invitation pays the bill. Businesswomen expect for businessmen to follow this rule.

- A handwritten thank-you note to your host is appropriate and should be sent within forty-eight hours.

Arriving at the Restaurant

• The host should arrive at least ten minutes early. The guests should be on time. Ten minutes late is considered rude. If you are detained, call and let the host know when to expect you. When you arrive late and others have ordered, start your order with the course being served.

• The host should check the table and request a change if the location is not satisfactory.

• It is proper to wait for your guest at the door. If coats need to be checked, the host should pay the coat fee and appropriate tip. (If the wearer of the coat would prefer to take the coat to the table, help your guest remove the coat if it seems appropriate.) The coat should be placed on the back of the wearer's chair.

• When the maitre d' leads you and your guests into the dining room, your guests should precede you in following the maitre d'. You lead the way if you are seating yourself and your guests.

• If you are expecting more that one guest, it is all right to be seated with the first guest, after waiting for ten minutes. Ask your waiter to show additional guests to your table. If you are the guest and arrive before your host, check to see if a table has been reserved in the host's name. If the restaurant begins filling up quickly, ask the table host to seat you and to direct the others to your table as they arrive. If your host has not arrived in fifteen minutes, you may order a drink. The table should continue to look untouched.

• Leave the table setting as is until all late guests have arrived.

• Always offer your guest the preferred seat, which is the one with the best view or which appears the most comfortable.

• It is still considered polite for a gentleman to assist a woman with her chair unless she makes an obvious move to seat herself. He does not have to rise each time she leaves or returns to the table during a business meal.

• Enter your chair from the left side and exit from the right

After Being Seated

• Pick up your napkin as soon as everyone is seated. Your napkin is on the left side of your plate with your forks. Place a luncheon napkin unfolded across your lap; a large dinner napkin is half-opened. The folded edge is placed towards your knees, with the open end positioned to catch the crumbs.

• The napkin stays in your lap throughout the meal. If you must excuse yourself from the table during the meal, leave your napkin in the chair rather than on the left side of your plate, as some people suggest. Do this because a used napkin has become soiled and unsightly as well as unsanitary. Why would you place that kind of used napkin next to your client's plate? The napkin stays in your lap during an after-dinner speech.

• The napkin is finally placed on the table, on the left side where it began, when everyone is ready to depart the table. If plates have been removed, place the napkin in the center where the plate was. Do not refold the napkin or ball it up.

The Ordering Process

• A waiter will offer to take orders for drinks at a noon or evening meal. Offer your client the opportunity to order. If he or she orders a drink, it is good manners for you to do the same. If either of you prefers a nonalcoholic beverage, there are several choices available, such as club soda, colas, and fruit juices.

• Most business people have gotten away from drinking more than one alcoholic beverage, if any, during lunch meetings. If a second round of drinks should be ordered, follow it with the food order.

• When passing anything around the table, move left to right – just as in reading a book. Start on your left and pass to your right.

• Give your guest some menu suggestions that will indicate the price range for ordering, or note what is good on the menu to indicate there is no price limit or preference.

• The host should tell the server that he wants his guests to order first. This lets the server know whom to serve last and who will be paying the check at the end of the meal. When you need service, quietly signal the waiter with your hand.

• Treat your server with professional consider-

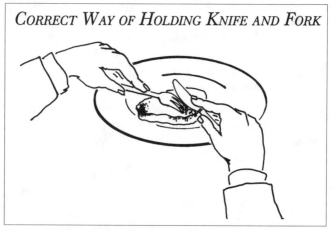

CORRECT WAY OF HOLDING KNIFE AND FORK

ation. A generous tip of 15% to 20% is a small price to pay when you receive excellent service, personal attention and the business that you hope you'll earn with your client. Figure your tip on the food cost before the tax was added.

The Table Setting

• Your liquids which include water, coffee, wine or iced tea are on your right.

• Your salad is on your left above the forks.

• Your bread and butter plate is above the salad plate.

• The cocktail fork may be nested in the soup spoon.

• A fish course will be served if the place setting includes three forks and at least two knives. The fish knife resembles a dagger and is obviously different from the entrée and salad knives. It is held like a pencil and is used to lift the fish meat onto the back of the fork tines, European style.

• Dessert fork and spoon may be placed above the dinner plate.

• Begin eating with the cutlery farthest away from the plate.

Correct Use of Cutlery and Other Objects

• Cellophane cracker wrappers and sugar packet wrappers may be folded and placed under the bread and butter plate to keep your area neat.

• Pass bread, butter and condiments to your right.

• Taste your food before salting it to avoid insulting the chief.

• Pass salt and pepper shakers together.

• When eating soup, the spoon is filled by moving it away from you, not toward you. The spoon exits the bowl away from you at the back edge. It is proper to tip the bowl away from you to get the last bit of soup in your spoon. If the soup is served in a cup with handles on both

Water Glass

White Wine Glass

Red Wine Glass

Soup Spoon

Cocktail Fork

Salad Knife

Dinner Knife

Dessert Spoon

Dessert Fork

Bread and Butter Plate

Butterknife

Dinner Fork

Salad Fork

THE
TABLE
SETTING

sides, you may pick up the cup by the handles to drink the last bit of soup.

• After being used, iced tea spoons may present a placement problem because coasters are seldom used today. I recommend that you gently shake any liquid from the spoon after quietly stirring the tea, and return the spoon to its original setting.

• When cutting meat, the knife and fork are held in identical hand positions. The handle of each utensil is placed in the palm of each hand with the index finger on top of the handle. It is not correct to grab the fork and wrap your fingers around the handle. Do not "stab the meat and saw it." Cut only one or two pieces of meat at a time.

• Bread is to be eaten in bite-size pieces and buttered as you eat. Keep the bread on the bread plate instead of putting it on your dinner plate.

• Pass the butter with the butter knife on the dish.

• Pits, seeds and foreign matters come out of your mouth the same way they went in. Fish bones are removed with the thumb and forefinger.

• Knife and fork handles should not hang off the plate (like boat oars in the water) when not being used. Keep the entire fork or knife on the plate.

• The "resting position" is made by placing the knife beneath the fork to form an X. The blade faces the diner. The fork is on top with the tines facing down. This signals the waiter that you are not ready to have your plate removed.

• When you are finished with your meal, place the knife and fork parallel to each other on your plate. The handle ends should be at four o'clock with the knife tip and fork tines pointing at ten o'clock.

• White wine glasses should be held at the base of the stem in order to keep the wine chilled. The same is true for champagne stems.

• Red wine and brandy glasses may be held with fingers on the bowl of the glass.

• Toasts should be made towards the end of a festive meal. It is an honor to be toasted. The person being honored with the toast never drinks to himself/herself. Simply acknowledge the honor with a smile and nod of your head towards the person presenting the toast.

• "Clinking " glasses is no longer necessary to a toast. It was done long ago to ensure that no poison or drug was in any one of the glasses. The clinking was done with enough vigor to cause a drops of liquid to spill over into everyone's glasses!

Do's and Don'ts

Do:

• Seat a woman on her escort's right.

• Be a good conversationalist during a meal.

• Sit up straight in your chair.

• When at a small dinner party, wait for the hostess to begin. If you are in a large setting with several tables, wait until every one at your table has been served before you begin.

• Raise your fork up to your mouth by lifting your arm. Do not lower your face to the table to reach the fork in a hand that is resting on the table.

• Chew your food with your mouth closed.

• Use your napkin to remove food oils from your lips before drinking your beverages. Lift your napkin to your lips and dab the napkin on your lips.

Don't:

• Don't inspect and freshen makeup at the table during a business meal/appointment.

• Don't begin eating before the host or hostess begins.

• Don't turn a wine glass upside down to indicate that you do not want wine. Simply place your hand over the top of the glass to signal "No" to the waiter as he offers to serve you wine.

• Don't use your napkin to blow your nose at the table. Go to the restroom.

• Don't pick your teeth at the table with a fingernail. Don't walk out of a restaurant using a toothpick. Use toothpicks out of the public eye.

• Don't "table hop" and interrupt others' conversations.

• If a telephone conversation is unavoidable, make the call away from the table. Do not carry your mobile phone to the table unless it is critical to the business at hand.

• Don't invite a superior to lunch or dinner. It is up to him or her to issue the invitation.

• Don't smoke at the table during the food order process or between courses. The only acceptable time to smoke at the table is after dinner, during coffee. Always ask permission of those sitting next to you. Some people are allergic to cigarette or cigar smoke and will have an immediate problem with nasal congestion.

CONVERSATION GUIDELINES

Cocktail Party

This is not the place to initiate a serious business conversation. It might be appropriate to set up a business meeting in the future.

Business Breakfast

This meeting is often one hour or less. Business may begin once the first cup of coffee has been served.

Business Lunch

Business may begin after the food order is taken. Make a smooth transition from small talk to business talk. Humor is a great tool.

Dinner

Keep business topics to a minimum. This time is best used to get to know one another and spouses, if they are present. Better allow at least thirty minutes for socializing. It is the responsibility of the host to initiate the business conversation.

Host's Responsibilities for Dinner Conversation

Introduce everyone to one another. Provide enough information to promote a conversation that begins naturally. Initiate the business conversation. Keep the emotions of the group compatible.

Thank-You Note

A handwritten thank-you note is appropriate after you have been a guest for a meal. If your handwriting is illegible, type the letter. Send the note within forty-eight hours, so that you do not forget. When using a fold-over informal note, open the note and begin writing on the lower half of the page beneath the fold. The back of the note may be used for completing the message.

"The significant problems we have can not be solved at the same level of thinking with which we created them."

-Albert Einstein

Chapter Six

INTERVIEWS, APPOINTMENTS AND INTRODUCTIONS

6

Resumes

A resume should be treated as a vehicle to get you into an interview. Competition for the job you want can be very stiff. A well constructed and designed resume plus an effective cover letter is important. You will be selling yourself, your qualifications and your experience. Like the fifteen second first impression, your goal is to create material that will encourage the reader to finish all of your information.

When preparing a resume, learn as much as possible about the position you are applying for and about the company's mission and goals.

Professional writer, Sue Nowacki, suggests that a Summary Group at the beginning of the resume will attract the reader's interest. Highlight your personal and professional skills and characteristics.

The layout of your resume is very important. It needs to be professional in appearance with correct grammar and spelling. Use "bolding" and italics sparingly. Visual readability is enhanced through neat margins, adequate "white space" and indenting to highlight text.

Make certain that all of the information needed to contact you is clearly visible and at the top of your document. Your resume may be scanned, faxed or photocopied by those interested in interviewing you. Make sure that the paper you use will hold up.

The resume length should be one to two pages. Document your last ten years of employment if you have that experience. Current history will be valuable to entice the reader into wanting to meet you. A potential employer wants to see how hiring you will benefit him or her and the company.

Print extra copies of your resume and have them with you when you go to an interview.

Your resume was carefully prepared and has gotten the interviews you wanted. Interviewing for a job tends to give most people a case of nervous jitters. For the college graduate, a sparkling GPA and list of extracurricular achievements will usually earn you a shot at an interview. When the economy is sluggish and companies are hiring fewer new employees, you need to know how to make a very positive first impression. Knowing the basic rules of interviewing etiquette will carry you through the moment of terror, confusion, and excitement. The ability to display proper social skills is critical to the interview process.

Dress Appropriately for The Job Interview

There is no second chance when it comes to first impressions. A first impression is often made within twenty seconds of meeting. Pre-interview preparation means more than learning pertinent information about the company. You need to make an intelligent decision about what you will wear. Clothes may not make the man or woman, but they can make a difference in a job interview.

The first consideration is finding out what is suitable for the company. If possible, go to the company beforehand and do some " constructive snooping." This will show you first hand what the employees and executives are wearing. Do the men wear a three piece suit, or blazers and trousers? Do the women wear matching skirt and jacket suits and coat dresses?

- A classic suit in a traditional color of charcoal grey, navy or blue is always safe. Many women are wearing strong colors, such as teal, red, and purple, in some industries. Check it out before going for the interview.

- A man's necktie has a way of giving an indelible impression of its wearer's attitude, taste and status. A silk tie looks both luxurious and authoritative, and it is practically seasonless.

- Jewelry should be understated, simple and elegant. Avoid wearing anything controversial. Men should not wear an earring to an interview even if it is part of the dress "norm" in a particular industry. Wait until you get the job.

• Makeup should be applied carefully so that it does not look excessive.

• Demonstrate great attention to detail, from your haircut to your shoe shine. These details will be noticed, and they send a strong nonverbal message to the interviewer about your attention to detail.

When Does the Interview begin?

When you exit your car, you may be under inspection from an office window by the person you want to impress. Walk with a strong, purposeful stride into the building. Carry yourself erect and with your chin up and your eyes alert and forward-looking. If you are under observation, your body language will have just communicated that you are eager for the interview opportunity and your future employment.

Arrive ten minutes early. Treat the receptionist with respect! This person is between you and your interviewer. Ask the name of the person who will conduct your interview. While you wait, concentrate on the information that you have gathered about the company. Mentally review some of the answers to questions that you expect to be asked.

Remember to put forth the best you that you have to offer. Carry your briefcase or purse in your left hand. Greet the interviewer with a firm handshake, eye contact, and a smile, and use his or her name. Stay on the side of formality unless instructed otherwise. Be seated after you have been asked to sit in an indicated chair. Avoid starting the "small talk." Never use first names unless you have a friendly and long standing relationship with the interviewer. Relax and put your assets to work for you.

• Listen to your voice. Speak clearly and loudly enough to be heard.

• Keep your voice in a low-pitched register. This conveys confidence.

• Sit up straight and lean forward slightly to indicate interest.

• Be comfortable with pauses. You'll have a definite advantage if you can use silence wisely.

• Don't be afraid to show your humorous side when appropriate.

Questions to Expect

You should expect certain questions to be asked by the interviewer. Formulating your answers prior to the interview will bolster your self-confidence. Practice your answers by using a tape recorder to critique yourself. Your life and work experiences, family history and background, skills and knowledge base, as well as the ability to change are of vital interest. What answers would you give to the questions below?

• Did you have to work while attending college?

• Did you pay as much as fifty percent of your college cost?

• What kind of experience do you have in getting along with people?

• What kind of job are you interested in?

• Why do you want to work for this company?

• Why do you think that you can do this job?

• What skills have you developed that you feel would be helpful to you in this job?

• What are your career objectives? What job do you expect to have in five years?

• What is the most difficult decision you've had to make recently?

• What would your previous employer have to say about your performance?

• Why did you leave your last job?

• What do you feel are your greatest strengths ? Weaknesses?

• What do you know about this firm?

The next group of questions comes from a newspaper article, "The Myers Report," by Gary Myers.

- What are the two most stressful experiences you've had in your life? What impact have they had on your life?
- What are the greatest challenges you've faced in your work life? The greatest success? How did each come about and what did you learn?
- What is the biggest barrier you've overcome, either personal, professional or social in the last year?
- What kind of study habits did you have in school? Describe your work style.

It is illegal to ask you about your ethnic origins, your religion, your age, your marital status, or your plans for having children. You do not have to answer personal or financial questions.

The New Interview

The interview process has undergone some changes according to Nicholas Corcodilos, the director of an executive search and consulting firm. He says that the new interview "is a hands-on, at work meeting with an employer who needs to get a job done and a worker who is fully prepared to do the job during the interview."

Job applicants have to do their homework in order to demonstrate an understanding of who the company is and some of their strategic and tactical problems. The interviewer may describe a situation and ask the candidate how he or she would handle it. The purpose of this tactic is to watch how the candidate tackles and solves business problems. During this process, the candidate should talk about how they have tackled similar assignments in the past and the business tools they bring to work out the solution to the problem.

The Interview is Over

When your interview has been completed, thank the interviewer for the time and make a positive statement about the process. Rise when the interviewer does, extend your hand, and call the person by name. It is appropriate to ask when you can call or when a decision on hiring for the position is expected.

A brief, handwritten note should be sent following the interview. Thank the interviewer for the time he or she spent with you. It is appropriate to end the note by saying that you are looking forward to hearing from him.

When you make it to the final interview, negotiate for salary and benefits. You should act confident at this point and be specific about salary and other financial options you will need. Most employers will mention club membership benefits at this time if they apply to you.

Introductions

Who is introduced to whom? According to Letitia Baldrige's *Complete Guide To Executive Manners,* there are definite guidelines to follow when making introductions in a business setting. BASIC RULE: Mention the Most Important Person First.

- Introduce a peer in your company to a peer in another company.

- Introduce a non-official person to an official person.

- Introduce a junior executive to a senior executive.

- Introduce a man to a woman unless he is the President or CEO and being introduced to the Vice-President, a woman.

- Introduce your supervisor to a client.

- When introducing members of the same sex, age, rank, and degree of distinction are guiding factors.

• Use a person's official title when talking to or introducing him, even if he no longer holds that position.

• Use a title and last name in introductions when you do not know whether it is proper to use the first name also.

• When introducing your friends to others, use first and last names.

• Call people by the name they prefer, not the one you prefer. Using incorrect names hurts your credibility.

• A married woman who uses her maiden name in business should make a point of emphasizing her husband's last name in the introduction.

• When introducing a widow, give both her given name and her late husband's name.

• When introducing yourself to someone you don't know, give your first and last names. Don't give yourself a title or honorific.

• "Ms." is no longer a controversial subject. Women who are not married or are married and do not want to focus on their marital status use "Ms." It is used in conjuncture with a woman's given and family name.

Remembering Names

"What's in a name? That which we call a rose
by any other name would smell as sweet."

- William Shakespeare

Remembering another person's name seems to be a constant challenge for most people. Seldom do you hear someone say, "I can always remember a person's name but I usually forget his or her face!" The ability to call a person by his name is a wonderful asset, but most people need some mental prodding to recall names consistently. Think of your mind as a computer, if you will.

• When you meet a person for the first time, listen with the intention of recording the name into your personal mental computer. Don't forget to press the SAVE key.

• Repeat the name aloud during the introduction. Use it again in the next couple of sentences.

• If the name is difficult to understand, ask that it be repeated. If it is an unusual name, ask the origin; comment on what a pretty or strong name it is. Ask any other question that shows your interest in remembering the name.

• If the name sounds hard to spell, ask for the correct spelling.

• Mentally linking the name to an object that will remind you of the name you want to remember is a technique many people use successfully.

Forgetting Names

It happens to everyone! When you forget, admit to a memory lapse and ask for help. However, people expect you to remember after one or two times of asking for help. After that, it appears you don't care enough to remember.

I do quick "self-talk" when I know that I know the name and it won't come out of my mouth on mental command. I tell myself that I have SAVED the name in my mental computer and that the computer is "booting up" slowly and the name is coming up soon. Then I engage in small talk until the name pops out of my mouth. This technique may not be technically approved, but it is working for me.

If you do not hear your name mentioned immediately in an introduction or greeting, it is safe to assume that your name may be escaping the other person's memory at that moment. Be gracious and offer your first and last name quickly as you offer your hand and a smile.

First Names and Nicknames

There is a right time and a wrong time to call people by their first names. When in doubt, do not call a person by his or her first name.

• A young person should wait for an older person to invite him to switch from the last name to the first name.

• In a business situation, use titles with distinguished clients.

• Use titles in referring to senior executives when making a business presentation before an individual or group of clients.

• Nicknames have a special meaning within a family and perhaps within an organization. Yet many nicknames do not fit well into a conservative business environment. Consider your nickname and whether it is too casual to be used in your business environment. Introduce yourself from the beginning by the name that best fits your business image.

Chapter Seven

OFFICE PROTOCOL

7

We form our first impressions of an office and the people who work there when we enter the door. We make our decision about the company image based on the furniture, carpet, wall treatment, art works and accessories that we see. We look at the receptionist, at how she is dressed and how she greets us. Every guest who enters an office should receive cordial and business-like attention.

Receptionist and Waiting Area

Receptionists do not stand and shake hands when a guest comes into the office. They do, however, need to look up from their work, smile, make eye contact, and listen to what is being said. A positive first impression is made this way.

The receptionist will notify the person whom the guest has come to see and offer the guest a beverage if it is appropriate. She also will indicate where a wet umbrella may be stored. A variety of current magazines and a telephone for the guest's use while waiting make the area comfortable. Entertaining guests is not one of the responsibilities of the receptionist. When escorting the guest to another area, the receptionist always takes the lead.

Office Greeting and Seating

Welcome your guests into your office as you would into your home. Come to them if you are behind your desk, smile as you extend your hand, greet them with warmth, and call them by name.

The handshake is the universal sign of greeting in the United States and it is regarded as a gesture of good will. Men and women extend hands at the same time.

What is the message conveyed by handshakes? The half-handshake is regarded by many people as weak, while the "bone-crusher" grip indicates lack of sensitivity and a need to dominate. A firm handshake with hands parallel to each other and inserted fully into the space between the thumb and index finger creates a positive impression.

Hugs and kisses are not appropriate greetings in office settings or at business dining meetings. Double-clasp handshakes or arms around necks or shoulders are considered overly familiar gestures in most situations.

However, in some parts of the United States, people with a warm, open attitude will use a double-clasp shake with friends or they will place one hand on the upper arm while shaking hands. Always stay conscious of the body language of those around you and respect their personal space.

Seating

As a gracious host, indicate to guests where they are to sit. If the guest has an overcoat, indicate where it may be put. A well-mannered guest waits for the invitation to be seated. A guest keeps a briefcase or purse on the floor or in the lap, not on the host's desk.

Leaving

When business is concluded, the host should escort the guest back to the main exit, use the guest's name, thank him for coming, and conclude the visit with a handshake and eye contact.

"Remember that your office is up for scrutiny as are the manners you exhibit in the office."

-Jan Yager

WORKING ATMOSPHERE

"Courtesy is contagious. Catch it while you can. It's the key to the corner office."

- Valerie Sokolosky

Keep the hallways of the office clear. Do not congregate to exchange pleasantries or discuss business. Your voices could be disturbing to those working and they might overhear something that is not their business to know.

Doors should be used as a nonverbal communication tool. A closed door means KNOCK and WAIT to be invited to enter. An open door signals that it is all right to come in. However, it is courteous not to start speaking if the person is talking on the phone when you enter his office.

Walls are thin in many office buildings. Monitor what you say and how you say it. Be aware that your voice could be traveling through walls and annoying those conducting business next to you.

"Do unto others as you would have them do unto you."

-The Golden Rule

• Put it back where it belongs.

• Indicate a reorder if you use the last one of anything.

• Keep the coffee pot and refrigerator area clean.

• Start the next pot of coffee if you pour the last cup.

• Be respectful of others' time.

• Refill the paper tray in the copier.

• Return the copier to "normal" if you alter the setting.

• Don't eavesdrop on others' conversations.

• Never put someone down in front of others.

• At work, smile and acknowledge one another as talented people.

"Do unto others as they would like done unto them."

-Platinum Rule

OFFICE MEETINGS

"Executives spend 25% to 70% of their day in meetings and consider about a third of those meetings to be productive."

-USA Today

When people are arriving for a meeting, there may be moments of uncertainty between business women and men. Gender is no longer an issue when a group of people enter an elevator. Men do not need to let the women enter first. That courtesy usually places women in the back of the elevator, which then causes a shuffle as the men move around in order to let the women exit first. The persons closest to the door exit first.

Most businesswomen in the '90s prefer to open their own car and office doors. The person who reaches the door first may open it for the others. The person without packages opens the door for those who are burdened with packages. Men who are in the habit of extending social courtesies to women often have difficulty in changing these courtesies. A woman should be gracious and thank the man who extends the courtesy, then state her preferences.

Arrive on Time

It is a good idea to arrive several minutes ahead of the scheduled time for an important meeting. If you know that you will be detained, call ahead to alert the chairman as to when you should be arriving. A meeting should start at the stated time, out of respect to those who arrived on time.

Introductions and Greetings

Before the meeting starts, greet those around you whom you know. Try to shake hands with the most senior person first. Deference to elders is always considered appropriate. Introduce yourself to those you do not know. If you are a newcomer to a group, listen to hear whether people are using titles and last names, or whether everyone is on a first name basis. It is better to err to the side of formality the first time.

If names tags are used, place yours on your upper right shoulder for easy identification.

The manners of the meeting chairperson should be exemplary, setting the tone for the meeting. The chairperson sits at the head of the table and the main door of the room should face the chairperson. The seats to the right and left of the chairperson are for that person's peers and honored guests.

Position Yourself

Make your seating location work for you. When two people are having a meeting, position yourself to your colleague's right, with a bit of space between you. When there are more than two people present, position yourself to the right of the chairperson, where you can see the faces and reactions of the others present. If you are a junior member at the meeting, always wait for the senior person to indicate seating. Use this rule when you are in a conference room, an executive's office, a restaurant, or a limousine.

Be Prepared

If you are chairing a meeting, have a typed agenda with a copy for each person present. Someone should take minutes of what goes on in a meeting.

If during the meeting you are making a presentation that requires the use of audiovisual and electrical equipment, arrive early enough to make sure the machines are working properly and are set up where you need them.

If any reading materials were sent to you before the meeting, read them. Be prepared when you arrive, and be ready to contribute to discussions. If you need to record what is said during the meeting, always ask permission from the chairman.

Respect Personal Space

When meeting around a conference table, be considerate of those seated on either side of you. Keep your papers in front of you, in your lap, or on the floor beside you. Human beings are territorial and are uncomfortable when people get into "their space."

If you are a smoker, choose a seat where others will not be bothered by the smoke. To decide if you may smoke, check whether the person in charge of the meeting is smoking. It is advisable not to smoke if the chairman is not smoking.

Effective Communications

"Speak clearly, if you speak at all; carve every word before you let it fall."

-Oliver Wendell Holmes

Quality, volume, inflection, and rate are all components of a good speaking voice. Your voice is an important ticket to take to a meeting and use effectively. You can inspire, energize, and organize those present by being aware of how your voice sounds. Make sure that others can hear you by using the volume appropriate to the group. Avoid inflammatory language and slang words, which do little to enhance your personal image.

Listening

Listen with the intent to learn. Active listening is the highest compliment we can pay each other. Listening communicates that we value each other's thoughts and words. Listening goes beyond the hearing process. It includes visual responses that let the speaker know that he/she is connecting with your brain. Use your facial expressions to indicate your mood of agreement, frustration, happiness or anger. Lean forward to show interest.

Do not interrupt a speaker. Even when you do not agree, wait until he has completed the sentence before you begin to speak. Respect for each person's feelings and time is critical when attending a meeting, whether you are a participant or the chairman.

"Nothing is ever lost by courtesy. It is the cheapest of pleasures, it costs nothing and it conveys much. It pleases him who gives and him who receives, and thus, like mercy, it is twice blessed."

--Erastus Wiman

Working Late

With increasing work loads, more people are coming to the office early and staying late. Follow these seven tips to stay safe:

1. Attach a sticker to your telephone listing the numbers of building security, the police and fire departments. Program the numbers into your phone if possible.

2. When signing a lobby ledger, use only a first initial with your last name.

3. Turn on the lights in main areas and in a few offices to give the impression that more people are around.

4. If you encounter anyone who looks or acts suspicious, call the building security immediately.

5. Avoid stairwells and dead-end corridors. Don't get on or stay in an elevator with someone who makes you feel uncomfortable.

6. Let someone at home or a neighbor know that you are working late and about what time you expect to be home. Let them know if you will be later.

7. Take the same route home if possible. That way it will be easier for people who are expecting you to find you if you are late with car trouble. Carry a cellular phone if you have one or if you do not have a phone installed in your car.

Chapter Eight

ELECTRONIC COMMUNICATION ETIQUETTE

8

When Alexander Graham Bell invented the telephone in the late 1800's, he had no way of knowing how complex that instrument would become by the late 1900's. "Surf the net" would not have meant to him what it does to us today. There is a new code of electronic manners in using the many instruments available for office and home use.

Telephone Etiquette

Seventy-five to eighty-five percent of today's business is conducted on the telephone. Ninety percent of the impression formed during a one-time call to an office is based on the voice of the receptionist or secretary. Your voice IS the first impression.

Courteous telephone communications include these twenty steps. Remember to:

1. Sit up straight, breathe deeply, talk into the mouth piece and smile. Put a mirror on your desk, look at yourself and create the face you would use if you and the caller were face to face.

2. Answer by the second ring.

3. Do not eat, drink or shuffle papers when you are answering and talking on the telephone.

4. Greeting - "Good Morning," - pause. This acts as a verbal handshake.

5. Give the name of company -pause - followed by your name. When a person gives their name, show that you listened and call the person by their preferred name.

6. Say "How may I help you?" or "How may I direct your call?

7. Pay attention! Callers should not feel that they are competing with other people or distractions for your attention. If a person comes in with an appointment, try to end the phone conversation or put the caller on hold until you have taken care of the visitor. Ask permission before putting a caller on hold at any time. Put a caller on hold if necessary, instead of covering the mouthpiece.

8. When you must leave the line, explain why and return promptly with an answer. A caller feels impatient if left on hold for more than twenty seconds.

9. React to a person's call with "Yes," "I see," or other appropriate phrases that indicate that you are listening.

10. Avoid slang expressions. Be professional. Do not call a woman "Honey" and "my dear" in a business call.

11. Repeat and record messages. Ask for correct spellings. Repeat the phone number.

12. If you get an angry caller, let them defuse before you try to assist them. Do not lose your temper because of their complaints.

13. Let the person who was called hang up first so that you know that the person you called has completed the conversation.

14. Always end a call with, "Good Bye."

15. Make sure that you return all calls in a timely manner.

16. If you have trouble reaching someone at work, ask when it would be a good time to call back.

17. When making a personal call to a friend who is at work, always ask if it is a convenient time to take the call. Keep your conversation brief.

18. If your secretary places your call for you and the person is available to take the call, you should be on the line when the person picks up the phone.

19. When your business calls do not come through a switchboard or a secretary, answer your phone with a verbal handshake followed by your name. Beginning with, "This is Robert" is too abrupt.

20. Be as positive as possible in your phone conversation. Close on a positive note. People remember what was said last.

The Answering Machine and Voice Mail

It was once considered rude to have an answering machine. Now people wonder how many more rings they have to wait through until they get a recorded voice. It is estimated that about sixty percent of U.S. households have an answering machine. Business people who office in their home also have voice mail which serves as an extension of the answering machine with more options. It is very frustrating to wade through a menu of options and never connect with a live human being. The following guidelines will help a caller's resistance to leaving a message when they get a recorded voice.

1. Use an answering machine that allows the caller to leave a long message.

2. When you record your message, smile as you speak, use a businesslike voice that is not high pitched and put energy into your voice. Listen to your message and keep recording it until you think that this is as good as it is going to get.

3. Change your office message daily if your schedule fluctuates. Let callers know when they can expect to reach you or receive a call back.

3. Change your office message daily if your schedule fluctuates. Let callers know when they can expect to reach you or receive a call back.

4. When leaving a message on a machine, state your name, phone number, purpose of your call and your request.

Fax Tips

The fax machine became an indispensable electronic communication tool for office and home use early in the 1990's. There are guidelines that are wise to follow whenever you choose this form of communication. Be considerate of the people in an office who use the fax machine and receive fax messages. Evaluate your message and ask yourself should it be sent by fax or by mail,

• When creating your "cover sheet," it is a good idea to include a line for the time and date. The sender data at the top of thermal faxes is sometimes cut off and the time gets lost.

• If you plan to fax a letter and do not intend to mail a copy, use a photocopy of your letterhead to write the letter on. This will save on the cost of using expensive letterhead.

• Faxes are considered more public than letters. Avoid personal comments that should only be for the recipient.

• If you plan to send a confidential fax, notify the receiver of the fax that the message is coming through so that the appropriate designate is at the machine to pick up it up.

• If your document is long, call the recipient, tell him the document's length and give him the choice of fax or mail.

• Do not use the fax to extend a last minute invitation. You appear to be very disorganized and it is considered rude.

• Think twice before using the fax machine for advertising purposes. Many offices treat these communications as junk mail and they are left unread and are trashed. Many machines have the capability to automatically and selectively block transmissions from about fifty junk fax offenders.

• Do not tie up an office fax with jokes for friends.

• Hand write your thank you notes, letters of congratulations, or condolences on good stationary. Do not use the fax for this purpose.

Netiquette

Netiquette is a set of rules for behaving properly online. When interacting with people via cyberspace, it is important to remember that you can either be friendly or offensive, depending on how you communicate electronically.

Electronic Mail

We are in the electronic age of global communication. Now, more than ever before we can reach out and communicate instantaneously with others across the globe. We can develop friendships, business relationships, and many networking opportunities. E-mail offers immediacy, convenience, multiple addressing and automated record keeping to those who want to communicate from one computer to another.

Think about how your message will read on the screen. Who might read your e-mail message? Who is your message for? Could your message be construed as negative? How would you feel if your message took an unexpected electronic turn and appeared in the wrong mailbox? Would you be better off using the telephone for a particular message? What is your "tone of voice" in your e-mail? Would you say the same words if you were face to face with the person receiving your message?

Remember that your message can easily be misinterpreted. Human warmth can not be conveyed by fax or e-mail. Reread your message several times before sending it. In this high tech age of electronics, remember that people appreciate the sound of the human voice. Before sending that e-mail, consider a phone call or a walk across the hall to the office for a human communication. The Golden Rule for cyberspace is as basic as: "Remember the human." Without the aid of the human eyes, voice and body language, your written word is all you've got.

Use the following tips when you send e-mail:

• Begin your message with a positive note. Do not start with a blunt reminder that the person is late in answering you.

• Save your funny remarks and jokes to use in a face to face meeting. If you think that one of your family members would be embarrassed if they read your message then you should not risk sending it.

• Make sure that your message is not too cryptic. People who use information control as a communication power play may find that their plan did not work out which puts them in an uncomfortable position or possibly unemployment.

• Be succinct. Limit your message to one screen if possible.

Rules For Proper Electronic Mail Use

There are rules of proper e-mail etiquette that must be followed in order to make the correct impression and to further the relationship across continents and cultures. Leah Woolford, BDSI, suggests the following guidelines.

1) Do not use e-mail like you might use direct mail. Some Internet users, especially overseas, must pay for each e-mail that they receive. By sending an unsolicited piece of e-mail you are forcing them to pay for something they did not request. This is looked upon as very bad manners on the Internet.

2) Make sure that your greeting in the e-mail is a bit more formal than you might otherwise use in a business letter. Many times an e-mail address does not indicate the country of origin for the sender, and in many countries the greeting and the tone of the letter will be better received if the tone is formal.

3) When replying to an e-mail, snip a short portion of the mail that you are replying to and include it in the bottom portion of your reply. This enables the reader to immediately remember the topic, and some details of the previous e-mail. Many Internet users receive hundreds of messages per week or month and this helps them sort out the topics until they become very familiar with you.

4) In the body of your mail, try to be polite and choose your wording carefully. Use of slang or jargon is not acceptable, especially in the international market where meanings can be different and sometimes very offensive.

5) Try to be concise with your message. E-mail is not the preferred method of a long document, unless it is "attached" to the initial short message.

6) Include full contact information in your signature if you are sending information for business purposes. The signature should include your name, company name, mailing address, phone and of course, the URL address of your web site if you have one.

• Spelling and grammar do count. Our written word is visual. Don't write all caps because it looks like you are screaming at the other person.

• You will be judged by the quality of your words. Be clear with your message. Say what you mean and mean what you say and do it politely. Avoid swearing. It is offensive to most people and won't win you many new friends on the net. Remember that your words could be saved somewhere and could come back to haunt you when you least expect it.

• Know where you are when you enter a domain in cyberspace. Don't rush into a discussion group without first listening to the language of the people who are already there and evaluating their mood.

• Respect other people's time and "bandwidth." When you send e-mail or post to a discussion group, be concise with your communication. Don't make the mistake of posting the same note to the same newsgroup six times. That data has to be stored and will take up valuable wire and channel space.

• Respect the privacy of other's e-mail. Just as you would not trespass into another's desk drawers or files, neither would you would read their e-mail

• Netiquette does include "flaming." Virginia Shea, author of *The Core Rules of Netiquette* , defines flaming as "what people do when they express a strongly held opinion without holding back any emotion." She says that flaming is a long-standing network tradition that can be lots of fun. However, when carried to the extreme, flame wars are an unfair monopolization of the bandwidth.

Be ethical. Do not lower your standards of behavior while in cyberspace. Do not take advantage of people just because you are not communicating face to face.

Chapter Nine

BUSINESS TRAVEL

9

Traveling is part of the job description for most professionals. The "process" of packing, buying tickets, arranging accommodations, getting cash, etc. requires organization on your part so that you minimize the stress frequently associated with business travel.

Basic Organizing and Packing Tips

• Check your ticket carefully before travel day. Make sure all dates and times are correct and that your travel club miles are credited.

• Check hotel confirmation slips to verify arrival and departure dates. A tired traveller who does not do this could arrive at a convention and find the hotel totally booked, which could necessitate his moving to another hotel.

• Store your tickets in the same place for each trip, so that time pressures and stress don't cost you a ticket that you misplaced.

• A good garment bag with lots of compartments and a sturdy shoulder bag can be carried on a flight, and can eliminate the need to check or wait for bags.

• An all-weather coat with a zip-in lining will accommodate you in most weather conditions. Include a small umbrella that will fit into your briefcase.

• Travel-size toilet articles reduce bulk. Pack liquids (shampoo, contact lens solution, etc.) in zip lock bags. Individual disposable toothbrush with paste packages are good to tuck in a pocket for an all-day business meeting.

• Portable travel-size hairdryers, irons, and contact lens heating units reduce bulk. Get a package of plug adapters for traveling overseas.

• Portable butane cartridge hair curlers are great. However, the butane cartridge is not supposed to be in the passenger compartment of a plane. I have had mine confiscated at security check when it was in my carry-on bag.

• Purse/briefcase size Mace receives the same treatment.

• A travel alarm lets you stay in control of your "wake- up" call. Carry extra batteries.

• Check your hotel exercise facilities and include that gear when a workout can be arranged.

• Combine trouser/skirt, blazer/jacket, tie/scarf and belt on one hanger to eliminate hanger bulk in garment bag.

• Pack outfits on hangers when using a suitcase.

• Fold shirts and blouses around tissue or laundry plastic bags to reduce wrinkling. Line the bottom of your suitcase with a plastic dry cleaner bag and place another plastic bag on top of the clothes before closing the bag. In case of spills, your clothes should be protected.

• Include a small can of Wrinkle Free and Static Cling.

• Tuck socks and coiled belts inside shoes for compact packing.

Brief Case Contents

• Business cards.
• Writing instruments - pen, pencil, highlighter.
• Legal pad for notes.
• Required reading and pleasure reading.
• Dictating machine.
• Walkman and headphones with choice tapes.
• Disposable toothbrush.

Cash to Carry

Begin With Fifteen $1.00 Bills For Tipping.

• $1.00 per bag to the airport porter when bags are carried from the entrance to the ticket counter. $.50 per bag to the porter who checks your bags in at the curb desk.

• $1.00 per bag to the hotel bellman who delivers bags to your room.

• $.50 per bag to the hotel doorman to assist you with bags into the lobby.

• $1.00 to the hotel doorman who hails your cab.

• $1.00 when Housekeeping delivers a requested iron and board.

• $5.00 to the concierge upon your arrival will insure good recommendations if you are staying for a few days. Tip for each service rendered.

• $1.00 or $.50 to bathroom attendant.

• $1.00-$2.00 per day left in your hotel room as accumulated tip in an envelope marked "for the maid," even if you never see her.

The Traveling Businesswoman

As a businesswoman traveling alone you may use your room for a business meeting and may eat alone in restaurants. There are, however, some basic rules to follow to make your time away from home safe and pleasant.

• The business image that you wish to convey starts with the way you dress, and it is reinforced by the way that you behave.

• Always begin a trip with an adequate supply of $1.00 and $5.00 bills. When checking into your hotel, identify yourself at the desk, tip the concierge for reservations and recommendations, and tip the bellboy well. Let it be known that you are on a business trip.

• In the event that you choose to have a business meeting in your room, remove all personal belongings except, perhaps, a framed picture of your family which might be placed on the dresser away from the bed. If papers have to be laid out on the bed, which is serving as a conference table, bring chairs up to the bed's edge.

• You may choose to eat dinner in the hotel restaurant, where she can control the environment. If you will be eating there frequently, tip the headwaiter $5.00, introduce yourself, and explain that you are staying in the hotel and will be dining there for several days. When entering the hotel restaurant or lounge, your posture and facial expression will tell others whether you are confident and comfortable about being alone. The *Wall Street Journal* or other business reading is a good accessory to carry and read while you wait for your order.

• When dining alone, make reservations with the restaurant beforehand. The better the reputation of the restaurant, the better you should expect the service to be. When dining at an exclusive restaurant, you are expected to tip 20% of the food cost, before taxes. Tip 15% of the cost of a bottle of wine in an elegant restaurant, 10% in a less formal one.

• Tipping is a reward or payment for good service. The percentages given serve as a guideline. The important question to ask yourself is, " Did the waiter really take good care of me through the service rendered to me?" If you are not satisfied, tip at least 10% and speak to the Maitre d' or manager.

• When you are having drinks in the hotel lounge with a group of people who are attending a conference that you are attending, be aware that if you are the last to leave, you may be presented with the bar bill. People who have contributed to the "running tab" but have left the lounge area may not have covered the cost. Be prepared with a credit card or a talk with the manager.

• If a man politely asks if he may join you for a drink, you may choose to invite him to sit down. If he pays for the first drink and you choose to stay for a second, make sure that you pay for that round. Also, make your time agenda clear and stick to it. It's a smart and safe idea to leave and return to your room alone after two drinks.

For Safety's Sake Traveling

Women traveling alone should never assume that they are safe. Be fully aware of your surroundings at all times. Some areas are safer than others. The hotel front desk, the coffee shop, and your room can be considered safe areas. When signing the guest register, consider using your first initial with your last name. Dangerous situations can occur in bars, elevators, parking garages, staircases and hallways. Carry a purse size, strong flashlight. Whenever you are out alone, walk with strong, purposeful strides and a confident expression. Look like you know where you are going and what you are doing.

Schedule your travel arrivals for daylight hours whenever possible. Always have your car keys out of your purse as you leave a building and head towards your car. When approaching your car in a parking lot or garage, look under it from a distance. Women have had their ankles slashed as they unlocked the car door by someone hiding under the car. Look in the back seat and on the car floor before unlocking the door. Get in quickly, and immediately lock the door before doing anything else.

If your return flight home is late at night, park your car in a well-lighted area close to the airport. If a person approaches you and asks for the time, look at his wrist to see if he is wearing a watch. If you choose to answer, keep on moving.

Wise Use of Travel Time Saves Time Later

• Place all receipts for cabs, hotels, and meals in one envelope to facilitate reimbursements and tax reductions.

• Review business meeting materials. Decide which papers to keep and which to throw away.

• Dictate draft correspondence in reference to meetings and/or conferences just attended.

• Take time to think and reflect on what you learned.

• Take time to rest.

• Take time to pray.

"We live in a wonderful world that is full of beauty, charm and adventure. There is no end of the adventures that we can have if only we seek them with our eyes open."

-Jawaharlal Nehru

Chapter Ten

ETIQUETTE IN **T**HE **G**LOBAL **A**RENA

10

There are many challenges to United States companies and individuals when they move into the global marketplace. The degree of success achieved between companies and people from different countries conducting business in the international business arena is improved when the diverse cultural beliefs, protocol and habits are studied and respected by all parties.

To Be A Good Global Guest

Learn how to earn the trust of the people where you will be traveling and conducting business. Learn as much as you can about the country, the people and their customs. People worldwide respond to others who observe basic protocol and demonstrate respectful behavior.

Americans are too often guilty of rushing into a new environment without studying the culture. Americans have had the attitude that the United States is the "center of the universe." This attitude does not work in the global marketplace. The world does not revolve around international customs, culture, language, and time lines. It is imperative to study our differences in order to handle ourselves appropriately in business and social situations.

• Ask your librarian to recommend current books about the country you plan to visit.

• If you know anyone who has lived in the country you plan to visit, ask questions about the proper business clothes you'll need to take and inquire about specific customs you'll need to observe.

Preparing for the Trip

• Will you need a passport and/or visa?

• A passport takes two to four weeks to obtain during a non-rush season. Rush services cost extra.

• Your business card proves that you exist as a professional person and business. Include your company name and your position plus any of your titles. Do not use abbreviations. If English is not spoken in the country where you will be conducting business, take your cards to a printer when you arrive and have the reverse side printed in the local language. Know the rules of business card exchange for the country you are in.

• Take an adapter kit and transformer for your electric razor, curlers, hair dryer and travel iron. Take a travel clock and extra batteries.

• Double- check all reservations for lodging the night before you are scheduled in each country where you will conduct business.

• Check with the local health department to find out if any inoculations are required in the country where you plan to travel. Allow enough time to have them if you need several.

• Take your medical prescriptions in labelled containers. Pack a variety of common over-the-counter medicines that you might use on a regular basis. It is very annoying and inconvenient to need a remedy in the middle of the night and not have it in your dob kit or make-up bag.

• Carry a foreign language dictionary for every country you will visit.

Cross Cultural Manners Matter

Rules of etiquette vary around the world. American travellers are often considered boorish in their behavior in other countries. Three principles should guide the American who is doing business internationally according to Lennie Copeland & Lewis Griggs, authors of *Going International.*

1. People tend to like and prefer to interact with people they perceive as similar to themselves.

2. Respect for etiquette is deep seated, deeper than we imagine.

3. Show respect.

A Few Important Differences to Understand

• The direct eye contact used by Americans is perceived in some countries as offensive. Not meeting someone's eyes directly while in other countries will mark you as a person who is shifty or dishonest.

• The firm handshake practiced by American business men and women does not apply universally when meeting people in other countries.

• It is very important for Americans to study the customs involved in business-related gift giving. A business relationship can get off to a bad start or even eliminate the opportunity to begin business because the gift was considered offensive in that particular culture.

• Female executives should find out about the appropriateness of giving a gift that is suitable for a man's wife and family as well as for the man with whom she will be conducting business. On the other hand, know which countries consider it rude to even acknowledge that a man has a family.

• Flowers are a universally accepted gift around the world. Use a competent florist in the foreign city whenever possible. Faux pas are committed when you do not know the guidelines relating to numbers, colors and types of flowers to send for each occasion.

• Eating and drinking customs and etiquette vary around the world. Graciously accepting the food served to you is tantamount to acceptance of your host, their country and the company. In some countries, your stamina to drink alcohol with your hosts will be tested. If you cannot drink at all, offer a medical excuse. That is the only valid excuse that will be accepted where alcohol is part of the social ritual.

• People have different relationships with personal space. When standing and talking with

85

people from another country, be aware of their comfort zone. Some will stand so close that you want to move away. Don't - they will follow.

• Make an attempt to speak a few phrases in the language of the country where you conduct business. Your effort will be acknowledged and appreciated. If you are not fluent in a foreign language and English is not their first language, make sure that an excellent interpreter is engaged for you. Your success could depend on this.

• If you are working with people who do not use English as their first language speak slowly and enunciate well. Be careful not to sound like you are talking down to people, especially when they are well-educated and have to take time to mentally convert languages. Listen to the volume of your voice. Americans tend to shout at people from other countries when communications are difficult. Speaking in a loud tone of voice does nothing to improve the language barrier.

• Avoid idioms and slang words and phrases. They can be taken literally by people whose first language is not English and will not mean the same thing in their translation.

• Gestures are as important and as easy to misinterpret as words. Hand signals used in America such as the "thumbs up," V for victory, and the circled thumb and forefinger are viewed as vulgar gestures in other countries.

• Don't be upset if people from other cultures show little reaction as you speak. Evaluate your jokes before telling them - humor doesn't translate well. Our puns and our sarcasm are not understood in other countries.

• Don't be surprised if people from other cultures are reluctant to ask questions. They want to avoid looking stupid in front of their colleagues. They also place high value on "face" and don't want you to "lose face" if you don't know the answer to their questions.

• What you wear for business and pleasure in an other country is important. You will need to blend into their environment - not accentuate your differences. You are a representative of your country and your company.

• Cigarette smoking is a major health issue in the United States. There are nonsmoking rules in airplanes, office buildings and restaurants. This is not the case in most other nations. Do not try to reform your hosts about smoking when staying in their country.

The points briefly covered in this chapter are meant to convey the importance of doing your own in-depth research on the etiquette and culture of any foreign country where you will spend time and conduct business.

In Summary

Manners must become an integral part of your daily behavior and habits. No one was born knowing how to act properly. Good habits are formed by repetitive practice.

Studies tell us that it takes twenty-one consecutive days to make or break a pattern of behavior. As you begin your morning, make conscious decisions about how you want to be perceived that day in your professional and social environments. Review your performance at the end of the day. Ask yourself: "Where was I effective? Where do I want and need to improve?"

It is in your best interest to master business etiquette. Partner it with ethical behavior. Gallup Polls have shown that public confidence in the integrity of business people is on the decline. Americans seem to be lowering their standards of what is morally acceptable in business and in politics. In *The Power of Ethical Management,* by Dr.Kenneth Blanchard and Dr.Norman Vincent Peale, they state that being ethical is good business not just because it is the right thing to do, but also because it results in a more successful operation.

Be a person who is known for excellence. Set high standards for yourself professionally and personally in etiquette and ethics.

> "The quality of a person's life is in direct proportion to his commitment to excellence, regardless of his chosen field of endeavor."

> *-Vincent T. Lombardi*

References

CORPORATE PROTOCOL

        by Valerie Grant-Sokolosky

BUSINESS ETIQUETTE AND PROFESSIONALISM

        by M. Kay duPont

The concise guide to EXECUTIVE ETIQUETTE

        by Linda & Wayne Phillips

POWER AND PROTOCOL FOR GETTING TO THE TOP

        by J.P. Davidson

SUBTEXT

        by Julius Fast

ELEPHANTS DON'T BITE

        by Vernon Crawford

EXECUTIVE ETIQUETTE

        by Stewart and Faux

NEW COMPLETE GUIDE TO EXECUTIVE MANNERS

        by Letitia Baldrige

THE NEW MANNERS FOR THE '90s

        by Letitia Baldrige

TELEPHONE COURTESY & CUSTOMER SERVICE

        by Lloyd C. Finch

UNLIMITED POWER

        by Anthony Robbins

HOW TO WORK A ROOM

        by Susan Roane

MASTERING BUSINESS ETIQUETTE and PROTOCOL
    by National Institute of Business Management, Inc.

DO'S and TABOO'S Around The World
                        by The Parker Pen Company

SPECTRUM MAGAZINE 1991 Volume Two

COMMUNICATION BRIEFINGS October 1989

BUSINESS PROTOCAL: HOW TO SERVICE & SUCCEED IN BUSINESS
                        by Jan Yager

NOTES

NOTES

NOTES

NOTES